D1123874

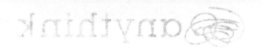

INHERITANCE AND VARIATION OF TRAITS

ROSE PEMBERTON

PowerKiDS press™

NEW YORK

Published in 2017 by The Rosen Publishing Group, Inc.
29 East 21st Street, New York, NY 10010

Editor: Melissa Raé Shofner
Book Design: Michael Flynn
Interior Layout: Reann Nye

Photo Credits: Cover, p. 17 Kris Wiktor/Shutterstock.com; p. 5 lostbear/Shutterstock.com; p. 6 https://commons.wikimedia.org/wiki/File:Carl_von_Linn%C3%A9.jpg; p. 7 Polarpx/Shutterstock.com; p. 9 everydoghasastory/Shutterstock.com; p. 10 Authenticated News/Archive Photos/Getty Images; p. 11 Buppha/Shutterstock.com; p. 15 Julija Sapic/Shutterstock.com; p. 18 Sherrod Photography/Shutterstock.com; p. 19 Microgen/Shutterstock.com; p. 20 https://commons.wikimedia.org/wiki/File:Darwin_Tree_1837.png; p. 21 Kingarion/Shutterstock.com.

Cataloging-in-Publication Data

Names: Pemberton, Rose.
Title: Inheritance and variation of traits / Rose Pemberton.
Description: New York : PowerKids Press, 2017. | Series: Spotlight on ecology and life science | Includes index.
Identifiers: ISBN 9781499425697 (pbk.) | ISBN 9781499425727 (library bound) | ISBN 9781499425703 (6 pack)
Subjects: LCSH: Genetics--Juvenile literature. | Reproduction--Juvenile literature.
Classification: LCC QH437.5 P46 2017 | DDC 576.5--dc23

Manufactured in China

CPSIA Compliance Information: Batch #BW17PK For further information contact Rosen Publishing, New York, New York at 1-800-237-9932.

CONTENTS

CHAPTER ONE

A COMMON GOAL

Our planet has many kinds of plants and animals. One thing they all have in common is the need to reproduce. Plants and animals reproduce so that offspring, or babies, can carry their **species** into the next generation. If organisms didn't reproduce, their species would go extinct, or die out. This makes reproduction a necessary part of an organism's life cycle.

Offspring may look a little like one parent and a little like the other. This is because they inherit, or receive, half their traits, or features, from each parent. No two organisms are identical, or exactly the same, which creates **variation** within a species. Even twins have differences as a result of their surroundings.

Variety within a species means that some individuals will be better suited for survival than others. These individuals will have a better chance of reproducing and making sure their species lives on.

These kittens can help their species survive into the next generation.

CHAPTER TWO

WHAT IS A SPECIES?

There are millions of plants and animals on Earth. In 1735, Carl von Linné created a system to organize all of these organisms. This **classification** system groups organisms with similar traits together. The biggest groups are very general, but the groups get smaller and more **specific** as you move through the system.

Species is one of these groups. As scientists learn more about living things on Earth, the meaning of "species" continues to change. Today, many scientists consider a species

CARL VON LINNÉ

Swans, ducks, and seagulls are all birds. They have many things in common but they aren't alike enough to be considered the same species. They can't breed with each other either.

to be a group of organisms whose members are able to breed with each other and produce offspring that are also able to breed. Two organisms of the same species can reproduce, but two organisms of different species cannot.

However, sometimes scientists group organisms into species based on the traits they get from their parents. Living things with a very similar set of features are grouped together as a species.

CHAPTER THREE

GENE BASICS

Genetics is the study of how **genes** control the features of animals and plants. Genes are found within the cells of an organism. They carry information about how an organism should look, grow, and behave. An organism inherits its genetic information from its parents.

The scientists who study genes are called geneticists. Geneticists want to know more about heredity, which is how organisms pass traits to their offspring through their genes.

Some of the genetic information that is passed on is for physical traits. These are traits that have to do with the body, like a rabbit's fur color or a plant's leaf shape. Behavioral traits are also inherited. These traits control how an organism acts. For example, a border collie puppy inherits the **instinct** to herd livestock from its parents. Traits for certain medical conditions, such as deafness in Dalmatians, can also be passed from parent organisms to offspring.

This puppy inherited long ears from its parents.

CHAPTER FOUR

MENDEL, THE "FATHER OF GENETICS"

Gregor Mendel was an Austrian monk who studied heredity in plants during the mid-1800s. By experimenting with pea plants, he discovered patterns in the way certain traits were passed down from parent plants to offspring. Mendel used pea plants because they have simple traits that can be displayed in two opposite forms. This allowed him to control his experiments and make careful observations. Unfortunately, it was a long time before other scientists accepted Mendel's work.

GREGOR MENDEL

Mendel studied genetics and heredity with pea plants for eight years. He grew more than 10,000 pea plants during that time.

Some of Mendel's first experiments involved breeding long-stemmed pea plants with short-stemmed pea plants. This created offspring that were all long-stemmed. When Mendel bred two of those long-stemmed plants with each other, however, some offspring were long-stemmed and some were short-stemmed. By experimenting further, Mendel discovered that genes come in pairs, with each parent passing on half of his or her pair. Depending on how the inherited genes are matched up, offspring display traits differently.

CHAPTER FIVE

PUNNETT SQUARES

In 1905, an English geneticist named Reginald Punnett created a grid, or chart, to show the possible outcomes of various combinations of genes. This grid is called a Punnett square. Mendel didn't have Punnett squares when he was experimenting with pea plants, but they can be used to show why some of his pea plants produced short-stemmed offspring, while others produced tall-stemmed offspring.

First, it's important to understand that the letters on the grid represent **dominant genes** and **recessive genes**. Dominant genes have the most **influence** in the display of a trait. Recessive genes have little to no influence, unless two appear together. If two recessive genes are paired, then there is a chance their trait may be displayed. After many experiments, Mendel realized that some of his second-generation pea plants had a mix of dominant and recessive genes.

These Punnett squares show what happened when Mendel bred different types of pea plants. Remember that when a plant has a dominant (T) tall gene and a recessive (t) short gene, the plant displays the tall trait. The short trait will be displayed if there are two recessive genes (tt).

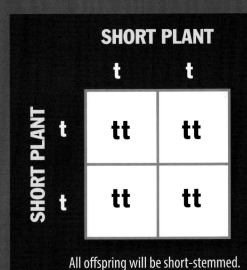

SHORT PLANT

	t	t
t	**tt**	**tt**
t	**tt**	**tt**

SHORT PLANT

All offspring will be short-stemmed.

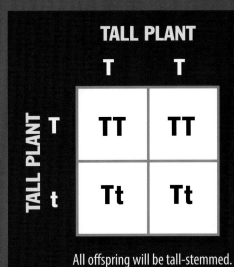

TALL PLANT

	T	T
T	**TT**	**TT**
t	**Tt**	**Tt**

TALL PLANT

All offspring will be tall-stemmed.

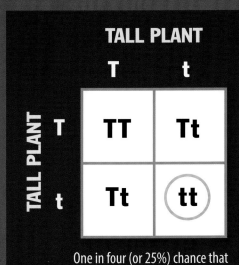

TALL PLANT

	T	t
T	**TT**	**Tt**
t	**Tt**	**tt**

TALL PLANT

One in four (or 25%) chance that offspring will be short-stemmed.

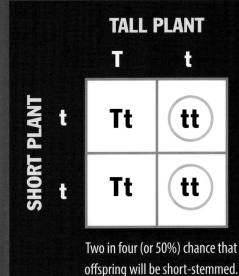

TALL PLANT

	T	t
t	**Tt**	**tt**
t	**Tt**	**tt**

SHORT PLANT

Two in four (or 50%) chance that offspring will be short-stemmed.

KEY
T = TALL (dominant)
t = SHORT (recessive)

CHAPTER SIX

INHERITED VARIATION OF TRAITS

No two living things are exactly the same because each individual has its own special combination of traits. This is called variation. One example is the differences between offspring of the same parents. A brother and sister might have different eye color even though they have the same mother and father. It all depends on how the genes inherited from their parents are matched up. Variation caused by genetics is called inherited variation.

Inherited variation occurs in both plants and animals. Mendel's pea plants are a great example. Inherited variation can also be seen in guinea pigs. Two long-haired guinea pigs could have one baby with short hair and a second with long hair, depending on how their dominant and recessive genes are passed down to their offspring. The variation within a species is always less than the variation between organisms of different species.

These baby rabbits are different colors because they each inherited different pairs of genes from their parents. The all-white rabbit with red eyes is called an albino. It inherited two recessive albino genes from its parents—a rare but not impossible combination.

CHAPTER SEVEN

ENVIRONMENTAL VARIATION OF TRAITS

Some traits are decided by genetic information. However, traits can also be affected by an organism's **environment**. The conditions surrounding an organism can cause a trait to be exhibited even if the organism didn't inherit genes for that trait. Climate, diet, exercise, and accidents can all cause variation of traits within a species. Sometimes **disease** also causes organisms to exhibit certain traits.

A genetically large animal, such as a polar bear, might be underweight if food is hard to find in its environment. A flower that is genetically supposed to have six petals will only have five if one petal falls off in a storm. A genetically short-stemmed plant might need to grow taller to reach sunlight if it's growing in the shade of a tree. Disease can change traits such as eye color or cause an organism to grow less than it's supposed to.

Identical twins, like these young jaguars, inherit identical sets of genes from their parents. However, their environment will likely cause variation in their traits as they grow.

CHAPTER EIGHT

CONTINUOUS AND DISCONTINUOUS VARIATION

The organisms of a species can display continuous and discontinuous variation of their traits. "Continuous" means "stretching on without interruption." "Discontinuous" means there are breaks or stops.

Continuous variation is shown in a species when there is a wide range of options for a trait. Height and weight

The body length of an alligator is a continuous trait because it could be any value between the length of the shortest and longest gators on Earth.

are features that show continuous variation. For example, giraffe height ranges from that of the shortest giraffe in the world to that of the tallest. A giraffe can be any height between these two values.

Discontinuous variation occurs when a feature of a species has a limited number of possible variations. In humans, for example, there are only four possible blood group types: A, B, AB, and O. There are no other possibilities. A human can only display the trait for one of these four blood group options.

CHAPTER NINE

NATURAL AND ARTIFICIAL SELECTION

Charles Darwin, an Englishman studying natural history, presented the idea of natural selection in his 1859 book *On the Origin of Species*. Natural selection is the idea that the organisms within a species that are best suited to live in their environment will be better at surviving. This gives them a better chance at reproducing and passing on the genes for those survival traits. Offspring inherit genetic information for traits that helped their parents to flourish. Over time, a species can evolve, or change. One species can evolve so much that it becomes an entirely new species.

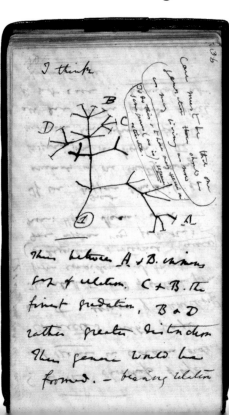

NOTEBOOK SKETCH OF AN EVOLUTIONARY TREE BY CHARLES DARWIN, 1837

Scientists have used artificial selection to breed tomato plants that produce more tomatoes.

Artificial selection is when a new kind of species is created using selective breeding. This means only organisms with certain traits are allowed to reproduce. Scientists use selective breeding to create plants and animals that are bigger, healthier, and better producers. They've selectively bred chickens to lay only certain color eggs and crops to be resistant to certain diseases.

CHAPTER TEN

GENETIC ENGINEERING

Today, advances in **technology** allow scientists to create genetic variation in plants and animals in the lab. Genetic **engineering** is the process of changing an organism's genetic code by adding or removing information. Genes from one species can also be added to the genetic code of an organism from another species.

Genetic engineering is used to alter an organism's traits. It's been used in scientific research, farming, and other fields. Scientists have genetically engineered crops, such as rice and potatoes, to grow better and be more nutritious, or healthy to eat. They've also genetically engineered bacteria and animals, such as sheep, to produce disease treatments.

Scientists aren't sure if long-term problems are created by changing an organism's genetic code. Some people worry it's unethical, or against what society thinks is OK. The benefits and consequences of genetic engineering remain to be seen.

GLOSSARY

classification (kla-suh-fuh-KAY-shun) A system in which things are arranged into groups.

disease (dih-ZEEZ) An illness or sickness.

dominant gene (DAH-muh-nuhnt JEEN) A gene that will always result in an offspring showing a specific trait.

engineering (en-juh-NEER-ing) The study and practice of using math and science to do useful things, such as building machines.

environment (en-VY-uhrn-muhnt) The conditions that surround a living thing and affect the way it lives.

genes (JEENZ) Many tiny parts in the center of a cell. Genes tell your cells how your body will look and act.

influence (IN-floo-uhns) The ability to convince others without using force.

instinct (IN-stinkt) The feeling every creature has that helps it know what to do.

recessive gene (rih-SEH-sihv JEEN) A gene that will result in an offspring showing a trait only if the offspring receives two copies of the gene, one from each parent.

species (SPEE-sheez) A group of plants or animals that are all the same kind.

specific (spih-SIH-fihk) Falling into a certain group with certain qualities.

technology (tek-NAH-luh-jee) A method that uses science to solve problems and the tools used to solve those problems.

variation (vehr-ee-AY-shun) Differences in the traits of an organism from others of its species.

INDEX

PRIMARY SOURCE LIST

Page 6
Carl von Linné 1707–1778. Oil on canvas. By Alexander Roslin. 1775. Now held at the National Museum of Fine Arts in Stockholm, Sweden.

Page 10
Gregor Mendel (1822–1884) at work in his laboratory. Photograph. ca. 1860s. From Getty Images.

Page 20
Darwin's first sketch of an evolutionary tree diagram. From "Notebook B: Transmutation of Species" by Charles Darwin. 1837. Now held at the Museum of Natural History in New York, NY.

WEBSITES

Due to the changing nature of Internet links, PowerKids Press has developed an online list of websites related to the subject of this book. This site is updated regularly. Please use this link to access the list: www.powerkidslinks.com/sels/traits